Platform
Papers

Quarterly essays from Currency House   No. 5: July 2005

CURRENCY HOUSE

PLATFORM PAPERS

Quarterly essays from Currency House Inc.

Editor: Dr John Golder, j.golder@unsw.edu.au

Currency House Inc. is a non-profit association and resource centre advocating the role of the performing arts in public life by research, debate and publication.

Postal address: PO Box 2270, Strawberry Hills, NSW 2012, Australia
Email: info@currencyhouse.org.au   Tel: (02) 9319 4953
Website: www.currencyhouse.org.au   Fax: (02) 9319 3649

Executive Officer: Eamon Flack
Editorial Board: Katharine Brisbane AM, Dr John Golder, John McCallum, Greig Tillotson

Shooting Through: Australian Film and the Brain Drain, copyright © Storry Walton 2005

ISBN 0 9757301 1 8
ISSN 1449-583X

Cover design by Kate Florance
Typeset in 10.5 Arrus BT
Printed by Hyde Park Press, Adelaide

THE UNIVERSITY OF
NEW SOUTH WALES

Lawyers

gleebooks

The publication of *Platform Papers* is assisted by the University of New South Wales, Holman Webb Lawyers (Australia) and Gleebooks.

From the Editor

With the present essay *Platform Papers* enters its second year of publication. Many sincere thanks to all those subscribers who have lent their support over the past twelve months; and to our generous donors who have shown their faith in what a year ago was little more than an idea. We have been very gratified by the extremely positive reactions, not only to the idea of a series of substantial quarterly essays devoted exclusively to issues in the performing arts, but also specifically to our first four essays and the problems they have addressed.

In publishing *Platform Papers* we have no agenda beyond that of Currency House's own mission, which is to assert the value of the performing arts in public life and the belief that such value deserves examination. It was never our intention to allow the status quo to remain unchallenged in these papers. The implicit directive to our authors has been to focus on an issue that in their view stands in need of urgent attention and to give them the freedom to address it. Issues that emerged last year were the ABC's declining arts programming, the changing world of the independent musician, the current structure of our theatre culture and the politically-loaded notion of mainstream values in the arts. We have encouraged our writers to be brave, well-researched, fair and fearless in setting down unpalatable facts and honestly-held opinion for public scrutiny. Criticism has been directed at principle, not personality, in the hope that a new direction or a pause for reflection might be seen to be in the national interest. We offer them as the subject of serious debate, a respected part of the national conversation.

A serious debate, however, needs two participants. So, should you feel moved to disagree with, question, challenge or correct what is written in these pages, you are invited—no, urged—to submit your thoughts in writing to our Readers' Forum, which is arguably the most important section of each paper.

Forthcoming essays will look at the new thinking of the Australia Council, at the economics of being an artist, and at structural changes in the music world. Being keen to build on what has been achieved so far we have, with your support, held our subscription price at a give-away $48 for four issues. So, stay with us and help turn what twelve months ago was a good idea into a thriving and profitable—in all senses of the word—enterprise.

John Golder

Contents

AVAILABILITY   *Platform Papers*, quarterly essays on the
performing arts, is published every January, April, July and
October and is available through bookshops or by subscription
(for order form, see page 70).

LETTERS   Currency House invites readers to submit letters of
400–1,000 words in response to the essays. Letters should be
emailed to the Editor at j.golder@unsw.edu.au or posted to
Currency House at PO Box 2270, Strawberry Hills, NSW 2012,
Australia. To be considered for the next issue, the letters must be
received by 4 August 2005.

CURRENCY HOUSE   For membership details, see our website
at: www.currencyhouse.org.au

Shooting Through

Australian Film and the
Brain Drain

STORRY WALTON

Author's acknowledgements

Background information and opinion for this essay have been generously provided by Rosemary Curtis, Carolyn Osterhaus, and Carole Sklan (Australian Film Commission), Mary Anne Reid (Film Finance Corporation), Judith Bowtell (Film Australia), Richard Harris (Australian Screen Directors Association), Megan Elliott and Claire Joyce (Australian Writers Guild), Warren Woodward (Australia Council), Professor Graeme Hugo (Adelaide University), Theo Newman (Australian Bureau of Statistics), Malcolm Long (Australian Film, Television and Radio School), Professor David Throsby (Macquarie University) and Terence Clarke (NIDA). I am most grateful to them all.

Producers, directors and other leading film industry people who kindly spoke to me for this paper include Gillian Armstrong, Tony Buckley, Barbara Chobocky, Kim Dalton, John Derum, Bruce Emery, Rolf de Heer, Tom Jeffrey, Lynda House, Phillip Noyce, Chris Penfold, Brian Rosen, Peter Thompson and Liz Watts. I extend particular thanks to each of them. Unless otherwise indicated, my sources for quotations, direct and indirect, are interviews I conducted with them in late 2004 and early 2005. Any faults of misrepresentation, of course, are entirely my own.

Finally, my special thanks to John Golder, wise editor and good counsel.

The author

Storry Walton, an early producer of arts programs for ABC-TV, has produced and directed many television plays and serials, including *My Brother Jack*. He has directed ABC documentaries on art and on rural matters and, while based in London, made programs for the BBC-TV social documentary series, *Man Alive*. He was Director of the Interim Training Scheme, the precursor to the (then) Australian Film and Television School, of which he was an early director. In the visual arts field, he was Executive Director of the International Cultural Corporation of Australia (ICCA). He has also had a long association with the National Institute of Dramatic Art (NIDA) as Chairman of its Academic Board and member of its governing board. In the music world, he has been Chairman of the Seymour Group, and a member of the Board of Management of the Sydney Symphony Orchestra. Currently, he works as a story consultant on documentaries, is a member of the Film and Broadcasting Industries Oral History Group of the National Film and Sound Archive, writes features on rural issues, and is a visiting teacher in the School of Visual and Performing Arts at Charles Sturt University.

A prefatory note

While the broadcast industry is much larger than the feature film industry, and it is essentially on television that most Australians see their Australian drama, this essay nevertheless concentrates on the film industry, because it is the flagship sector and because concerns about its structure, quality and diversity are most acutely evident at the moment. For reasons of space and focus, the influential power of Australian governments on the film industry is explored through the operation of the two Commonwealth Government agencies, the Film Finance Corporation (FFC) and the Australian Film Commission (AFC). An examination of the significant role played by the State Government film-funding agencies, and the collaboration between them and the national agencies, must await the attention of another writer.

In what follows the term *filmmaker* is used generically to describe directors, producers and screenwriters—and, although they are not the subject of specific examination, the creative disciplines of cinematography, sound and editing. And in the phrase *brain drain*, *brain* is understood to encompass imagination and talent, as well as intellect.

Introduction
Anxiety and flight

Last year, 2004, was an awful year for the Australian film industry. The number of films we made plummeted from a recent average of about 27 a year to just 15[1]—too few for us to claim we have an industry, or to provide a decent living for most filmmakers. This suggests a structural problem.

At the same time, Australian cinema-goers pretty well gave up on Australian films. We've rarely been an avid audience for our own films—the highest share for Australian films at the box office occurred in 1986, when, adjusted for today's dollar value, it was 9.5%—but last year it dropped to 1.6%, a record low.[2] It is still declining. Australians, it seems, do not like their own movies. This suggests problems of content, style and quality.

Critics and industry people say, with disarming candour, that we've been making too many crook films lately, and the word has got around. All the while, Australian actors and filmmakers are going abroad to live and work. They have been shooting through for a long time, but in recent years they have been doing it in increasing numbers. And the industry's recent woes have highlighted concern about their exodus. It is one thing to go away in order to test your mettle. It is another to go away because there is either too little work or no imaginative challenge to keep you at home. That's the rub. It suggests that Australian film may be in double jeopardy—of losing creative souls abroad for opportunity, and of losing those at home for lack of it. Could it also mean the direst brain drain is within? That we are allowing the native imagination and intellect of our film industry to drain away at home?

Behind this dilemma is our conditioned fear, wrought from years of battle, that if we let down our guard against the beguiling might of the United States film distribution and exhibition industry which has always dominated our screens, we will lose our film culture, and cease to see our own stories on the screen.

What is the future of Australian film against this backdrop of anxiety and flight? The film industry is not well, but the ailment is a temporary one. It is generally anticipated that 2005 will see some improvement. Henry Lawson, who played an interesting but little-known role in the pioneering days of our cinema, wrote that 'you can often see stars from the bottom of shafts in broad daylight'.[3] Taking its cue from Lawson and from people in the film industry itself, this essay looks upward through the gloom, to see how the industry is using tough times to make changes for a brighter future.

In Part 1, and throughout the essay, this path towards a brighter future is examined in the light of new studies of the brain drain, and of the recently identified phenomenon of the global circular migration of talent. It asks whether today's expatriation is a sign of chronic illness in the film industry, or whether it is something which, if mobilised, could be used to enrich the Australian cinema. To this end, Parts 2 and 3 discuss the kind of structural and conceptual changes which might so re-enliven our filmmaking culture, that Australian filmmakers might be more reluctant to leave, and when they do, yearn to return, at least from time to time. Part 4 considers the way in which the creation of an expatriate-return program might encourage the circulation of our international film talent through their homeland as a career imperative.

1

Brain Drain

Gone for good

For generations Australians have found 'overseas' to be a powerful lure. It is part of our national character, a function of our place in the world. It is endemic, this thrill for professional opportunity which drives you out against the fear that if you stay, your creative vigour will slowly die for want of exotic nutrients; against the conviction that if you stay at home you will be half-skilled, half-finished, half-realised. It is the universal dilemma of the provincial: to have your heart at home and your destiny abroad.

We have always felt ambivalent about the idea of ships and planes bearing away our talent. It has always betokened a fear of the loss of native imagination, or worse, of national intelligence. It has signified regret and guilt—regret at losing our brightest, and guilt at not having been able to keep them. It has meant pride in their achievements, and disdain, should they return without accolades—'They weren't really good enough, you know.' And it has caused puzzlement, when those we ignored or disliked looked back at us from the heights of international success.

The term *brain drain* was coined in the 1950s by the Royal Society to describe the loss at the time of cohorts of British scientists to the US—a one-way traffic and a notable loss of home-grown expertise. For Australians, however, *brain drain* has signified more than a one-way exodus. Few nations in the world have benefited more than Australia from other peoples' brain drains, especially after World War II, when our arts were enriched immeasurably by the migration from the old cultures of a ravaged Europe. It is a poignant image, that out on the high seas of the Indian Ocean in the 1950s and 1960s, south-bound ships carrying families propelled from post-war privations of their European homelands, passed north-bound liners crowded with bright young things from a peaceable and prosperous land, each shipload eager for the other's destination.

At this time, 40 to 50 years ago, artistically talented Australians left home for a variety of reasons. Ian Britain discusses a number of them in *Once an*

Australian. One of Clive James's reasons for leaving, he says, was that he had 'exhausted what challenges and comforts it could offer him'. And to the young Germaine Greer, 'the outward bourgeois decencies, the "even tenor" of suburban life, became an offence when unmatched, unrelieved, by any stimuli for the life of the mind'. 'I decided that Australia and I were deprived. We were boring', she said.[4] The artist Sidney Nolan, with whom I made a film in 1967,[5] told me that he had no option but to leave Australia to escape the stultifying artistic and critical environment. Yet he returned, with increasing frequency, 'to fill up the jug', as he called it. Even so, he remained suspicious about Australia: 'Don't let them get your kidney fat', he advised writers George Johnston and Charmian Clift, when they decided to return to Australia in the 1960s, after years of expatriation on the Greek island of Hydra.[6]

Later in the 1960s, when television drama, documentary and music were more active than the reawakening film industry, over fifteen directors left the ABC for London in the space of about three years, an extraordinary exodus.[7] As the film industry stirred, directors like Bruce Beresford, Fred Schepisi and Peter Weir also took flight. As I recall, they all went away for professional and artistic adventure, for ambition, to 'have a go in the big time', and to measure themselves against the highest standards. For the television directors, the magnet was London, because it was the international centre of excellence. Some film and television people left out of the kind of frustrations expressed by Clive James—the lack of challenge, their talent having outstripped what Australia could offer—or could cope with. And although most of the television directors returned over the course of many years, none I knew left Australia in the first instance with any sense that there would ever be anything stimulating and challenging to return to. As described later, that forlorn expectation seems to have changed for many of today's expatriates, who can move more easily between their international workplaces and their homeland, and even work in Australia occasionally without endangering their careers or putting them on hold.

For the most part, however, initial motives for embarkation, whether permanent or temporary, remain the same today as they were then. Those coming to Australia are in search of space and a healthier, more physical lifestyle. Most of those Australians who are leaving are in search of greater cultural diversity and professional sophistication. In the case of our filmmakers the destination is usually the United States.

For many Australians, however, the first experience of the brain drain was not overseas, but overland. My own experience of it, mirrored in that of countless thousands of others in other cities, began in Western Australia in the 1950s and 1960s. My generation knew the call of overseas well enough. As young men and women, we would lie on the beach at Cottesloe, facing westward out to sea, watching the mythic liners—*Orcades, Himalaya, Orsova, Stratheden*—take our clever and ambitious friends away to that nirvana where all imaginative life and labour found fulfilment, London. But behind us, across a desert as vast as any ocean, lay The East, the maw into which most young people were sluiced by the age of 25. Our compasses were set unnaturally to the magnetic East, because Melbourne and Sydney were where the head offices of most businesses were. And the losses were palpable. For years, Perth, like Brisbane, Adelaide and Hobart, was impoverished by the departure of its scholars, scientists and artists.[8] The major export of WA in those days seemed to be young people. It was a common sight to see knots of family and friends gathered on the platform of Perth Railway Station, to farewell their young leavers, about to be borne away by the *Trans-Continental* on their odysseys to the other side.

This overland brain drain continues today in the film industry. It is remorselessly and overwhelmingly to Sydney, where most of the film production companies, services, resources, agents and personnel are centred.

Today, however, the movements of our artists and filmmakers can be seen in a new global context, as part of a radical change in the migratory profile of all Australians. Graeme Hugo, who has been tracking our international working patterns since 1990, estimates that today there are nearly one million Australians abroad, three-quarters of whom are living and working on a permanent or long-term basis.[9] On a per-capita basis, this constitutes one of the largest expatriate workforces in the world. The number is unprecedented, and at 5% of our population, it is of sufficient size to be described, literally, as a diaspora. It is a manifestation of the increasing globalisation of developed economies. Its members are highly skilled and well-educated professional people at the peak of their careers, or in their early or middle years. Their economic significance is reflected in the terms used to describe them—'gold-collar workers' and 'cosmocrats'. What distinguishes this new migratory phenomenon is its mobility. Going from job to job means hopping from country to country while still working in the same field or with the same company. Unlike the emigrations of previous times, when people went away with little intention or hope of coming back, gold-collar workers typically circulate not only internationally, but back through their countries of origin, to which they return in passing. Some return for good. Australians return at a higher rate than do most populations—about 25%, compared with 11% of Americans, 15% of New Zealanders and 18% of British. Economists and geographers call it 'circular migration'. In a recent paper for the Lowy Institute for International Policy, Michael Fullilove and Chlo☐ Flutter gave the Australian movement a sense of life and energy. They called it a 'rolling diaspora'.[10] Australia's filmmakers are part of it, though to date they have been almost invisible in the data, as they have not been separately classified and tracked. Perhaps this essay will help to motivate their inclusion. They have been going away for years, but now some of them come rolling home—to work for a short while or to stay much longer. Many who have made successful careers overseas keep their homes in Australia. Some return to make films here. Unimaginable 30 years ago, this is a wonderful benefit of the global movement.

The rolling force of the diaspora cannot be stopped. Professional circles, think-tanks and governments around the developed world have accepted that circular migration is a fact of twenty-first-century economic life. Now, what matters is that we learn how to recognise it, understand it, and ask how its energy can be mobilised for the good of the home country—because, for all the philosophical acceptance of this global churn of the brightest and the best, there lingers in the international policies and emerging strategies of expatriation, the primal urge of each nation to hold its children to its bosom, together with the equally powerful desire to share economically in their globally enhanced expertise. Thus, Italy has its Directorate General for Italians Abroad, and reserves six seats in its senate for expatriates; Poland has created the Department for Polish Diaspora Affairs; Greece has its General Secretariat for Greeks Abroad; Ireland has its Ireland Funds; South Korea has its Committee for Koreans Resident Abroad and, since 1976, France has had its High Council for French Expatriates, whose councillors elect twelve members to the Senate. The British Government and the Wolfson Foundation recently established a £20 million research-award scheme to attract British scientists back to the United Kingdom.

What these world-wide activities of the private sector and governments have in common—and what should interest the Australian film industry—is the search for ways to keep expatriates in touch with home, to gain economic benefits from formal networking, and to engage them as professional and national advocates for business and the arts. Most important of all, however, if these ideas were to be applied to the Australian film industry, would be the need to encourage them to return home to work or to teach for short periods. As a reaction against the notion of departure and loss, these activities declare that *global* should mean home *and* away, and that some benefits of emigration and circular migration should accrue to the home country as well as to the receiving nations. Underlying all this research and activity is the hope that, when our bright stars go away, as they must surely do, their going can be for the good—of themselves, of their professions and of their home country. Gone for good.

To this end, Fullilove and Flutter recommend in their Lowy Institute Report, among other things, that the Australian Government should create a high-level unit within the Department of Foreign Affairs and Trade (DFAT) to develop and co-ordinate expatriate policies and programs as an integral part of national diplomacy. This would mirror the actions of many other countries with smaller diasporas than Australia's.

While the research activities of people like Fullilove, Flutter and Hugo, and others, have been vigorous, Australia has been slow to take an interest in expatriate policy at Commonwealth Government level. (The Victorian, NSW and Queensland Governments have already initiated, or are currently initiating, interest in the subject.) Things are changing, however. A Senate Inquiry into Australian Expatriates, set up in 2003, is due to deliver its findings soon. Its pithy terms of reference are pragmatic—and cultural—and include the direction to inquire into 'ways in which Australia could better use its expatriates to promote our economic, social and cultural interests'. The film industry appears to have made no submission to the Inquiry, but the words 'social' and 'cultural' should excite its interest. It could stand to gain from engaging with any outcomes of the Inquiry, and with the many research projects that are operating at the moment.

The Senate Inquiry attracted over 150 submissions, among them one from the Southern Cross Group (SCG). This volunteer-run and volunteer-funded international advocacy-and-support organisation for Australians working overseas shot to success within months of its foundation in Brussels in January 2000, and now has a committee network of 100 people in 30 countries and over 5000 website members in over 85 countries. While its volunteer base does not represent a model for a film industry expatriate program, which I believe will need professional services, there are four aspects of the SCG which should interest the industry. First is evidence of the extent to which it has tapped into the desire of Australians overseas to keep in touch with their homeland—personally and professionally. Would Australian filmmakers feel the same? Secondly, the speed with which the services SCG offers—of contact, information, advice, professional networking, advocacy, representation—have been taken up. Would filmmakers respond positively to the same services? Thirdly, the depth and breadth of SCG's information network and its submission to the Senate Inquiry. Is there information here which might be useful, if a film industry expatriate program were to be considered? And fourthly, the relevance of the 29 recommendations which SCG makes to the Senate Inquiry.

Three of the recommendations could be of special interest to the film industry, if they were ever to be taken up by Government. Recommendation 22 suggests government programs be established to develop expatriate knowledge networks and place people in Australian organisations. That sounds as if it could be translated to mean attracting filmmakers home for short periods of production. Recommendation 25 suggests the establishment of an umbrella organisation called the Australian Diaspora Council, to service the needs of Australians abroad and of Australia in relation to them. That could lead to diplomatic support for any program to bring Australian filmmakers home from time to time for production or teaching. Recommendation 29 suggests government support to establish a research facility in a University for the study of the Australian diaspora. More knowledge of Australian filmmakers working abroad could help strategic planning.

A proposal for an expatriate-return program is discussed in Part 4.

Gifts to the world

Phillip Noyce—director, notably, of *Patriot Games, The Quiet American* and *Rabbit-Proof Fence*—left Australia because he was fed up with running the gauntlet of the peer-panel assessment system of the various government film-funding bodies, and of what he remembers as the feast-or-famine cycle—long, empty breaks between intense bursts of production. 'I yearned to try myself out in a meritocracy', he said, 'where there were no peer panels, and no-one knew you, and you had to rely on the quality of your work, and your raw talent.' Talking of other expatriates, Noyce says that

Australians got work in America on the basis of

> the myth of the Australian personality. To Americans, we seemed to have the holy grail of human understanding. That, and practicality, having been brought up outside the studio system on films made for a fixed budget, we never went over budget. And we were versatile—we knew about cameras and sound because in a small industry you do all that as well as direct.

Over the past eleven years, for Phillip Noyce one film has followed another in regular succession.

Gillian Armstrong—director of *Little Women, Oscar and Lucinda, Charlotte Gray*, among other films—never thought she would go to America. It simply did not occur to her. So she was puzzled, when, after the success of *My Brilliant Career*, American studios kept sending her scripts to read. She left Australia, not propelled by frustration, but because she was summoned out of an innocent ignorance of the international stature of her own talent. Arriving in America, however, she quickly realised that Americans have an insatiable appetite, not only to read and see *anything* that might contain the seeds of an interesting film, but also to meet *anyone* who might hold the promise of originality and freshness. 'What's more,' she says, 'when you're young, you're cheap, so the opportunities are there to be given your first film.'

Lynda House—producer of *Proof, Muriel's Wedding* and *Ned Kelly*—explains further how talented Australians, directors in particular, not only answer the call of the industry overseas, as Gillian Armstrong did, but are propelled there by market mechanisms:

> Agents cherry-pick the very best. The last thing
> they want is a producer as part of a team, because
> the director is more valuable alone than attached
> to anyone else. Agents have these beautiful
> diamonds which they can cherish as individual
> talents.

House's own odyssey was to London, never doubting
that she had to go 'in order to keep growing'. 'I couldn't
get a competitive edge in Sydney,' she says. 'In London
you were always rising to meet the competition. It *is* a
production skill. I couldn't get it here, and London
was the only place where I could.' She missed Australia
dreadfully, and then, on her return some years later,
she missed the stress of the competition she had faced
overseas. She is thoughtful about the reasons people
leave:

> Many filmmakers have families, and the decision
> to uproot them for the USA, or, if you are
> established in America, to uproot them to return
> to Australia, are big considerations. It is not a
> simple thing. There are always other circumstances
> than wanting to go.

Brian Rosen, now CEO of the FFC, is one of only a
handful of Australians ever to have succeeded as a
producer in Hollywood. He revelled in the kind of
heady climate that Armstrong and House talk of, and
remembers with palpable excitement how the studio
executives 'were always breathing down your neck'.
They watched the film at every stage. 'They never
stopped asking questions, forcing you to think all the
time. They were always pushing your buttons.' The

professional energy of Hollywood kept him there for over ten years. What brought him back? The opportunity a high-level and influential position gave him to help re-invigorate the Australian film industry was a manifest attraction for him, and he makes no bones about the fact that 'Sydney is one of the best places to live in the world.' This lure of a good life is common to all expatriates, it seems. What finally convinced him to return to Australia, however, in the face of the serious problems the industry was facing, was the evidence, more clearly seen from a distance, of its potential: 'From the outside, with clear vision, I could see how many good things there were—good writers, good directors, good actors, top crews, tremendous government support.'

Australians have little difficulty finding work abroad because, as Brian Rosen notes, 'they are good, very good'. They are welcome overseas because of their high skills, freshness of attitude—call it lack of bullshit, if you wish—originality, versatility and irrepressible work ethic. *Star Wars'* producer Rick McCallum was unambiguous about his reasons for bringing *Star Wars: Episode II* to Sydney's Fox Studios: 'Australia has a powerful combination of talent and lifestyle factors that makes it irresistible. The acting talent is great and the crews are wonderful [...]. Nowhere in the world are crews so flexible.'[11]

It must be said at this point that the problems evident in the industry in the past two years are in no way attributable to any lack of skills or professionalism in the workforce. Indeed, the evidence points overwhelmingly, as it always has, to exceptional qualities. The problems, as suggested earlier, are structural and conceptual.

It is not possible say exactly how many Australian filmmakers are living and working overseas, because no centralised, systematic and comprehensive data on migration, employment or incomes are kept, which identify separately all film and broadcasting workers.[12] But the information posted regularly on the AFC's website gives an indication of who the people are that leave, and their numbers. For instance, the site currently lists as working abroad in film, mainly in the USA, some 90 actors, 28 directors and 12 cinemato-graphers.[13] Among nearly 120 NIDA graduates currently overseas, 33 are working, or have recently worked, in the film industry.[14] If these figures appear large, and their impact particularly remarkable, it is because the Australian industry from which this emigration flows is small. And there are more, of whom these figures take no account.

That the AFC cites the particular occupations of actors, directors and cinematographers is significant, for, with some exceptions, our film expatriates seem to be notably represented in the highly visible or high-end creative areas of the industry. In addition to those of Noyce and Armstrong, the names of independent directors such as Bruce Beresford, Jocelyn Moorhouse and Peter Weir spring quickly to mind.[15] Gillian Armstrong's reminder that 'the best films are director-driven' suggests that the loss of so much directorial talent is a matter of serious concern.

Among the high-end professions, film producers, however, tend not to go away. They stay in Australia, because, as Lynda House says, 'their savvy, skills and professional networks are deeply rooted in local knowledge'. Unlike the more portable skills of their colleagues, 'the expertise of producers is territorial'. Indeed, it makes it well nigh impossible for them to enter the production territory of another country. Brian Rosen and Sue Armstrong, who worked as producers in the USA, are rare exceptions. Both went away, and both returned. The Screen Producers Association of Australia (SPAA) knows of only one film producer currently working abroad. Fifty of the 600 members of the Australian Writers' Guild known to be abroad are working in theatre, television, childrens' programs and new media.[16] How many of these are working in feature film is not known, but it is probably a high number. The internet has obviated any need for some screenwriters to uproot themselves. Andrew Bovell, who currently has feature projects in development in America, and Laura Jones are notable examples of writers who work for production industries overseas, but have chosen to maintain their home bases in Australia. Claire Joyce is another: she lives in Australia, where she writes for Disney and production houses that make television programs for Central and Nickelodeon in Asia.

The digital revolution has also enabled talented Australians in the animation field, for instance, to set up their studio businesses at home and, at the stroke of a key, transmit their work to employers anywhere in the world. These internet professionals, whose work circulates in cyberspace, are creatures of the home economy. They export product from Australia and are paid in Australian dollars. But they are in the minority and give much less cause for concern than the larger numbers whose work is earth-bound, and who fly away to earn their living in worlds elsewhere. Behind an admiration for their brilliance and the concern at their flight lurks an uncomfortable question that is best whispered, in case it reaches the ears of the nation's economic rationalists: is something askew, when, at considerable cost to the taxpayer, the local industry and government develop Australian talents to nourish the Australian cinema, only to see them go and ply their trade offshore? Short of transforming our Immigration Detention Centres into Retention Centres, through whose gates the Government could cast any filmmaker who displays an interest in leaving the country, there is nothing to be done to stem the tide. Of course, there is an argument that we receive the benefit of our expatriates, value added, when we go to the cinema to see the performances of Cate Blanchett or Geoffrey Rush, or the films of Peter Weir and Jane Campion. If we prefer to dispense with the economic language, we can always regard them as national ambassadors and our gifts to the world.

Though the value of the creative spirit cannot be measured by economics, the question about the loss of so much home-trained talent persists, and it might well drive a closer search for programs which could plough back some of our expatriate expertise into the home industry.

Faith and oily rags

Everyone needs a healthy industry. Those filmmakers who stay here need it to be buoyant and entertaining to draw audiences and to be economically viable. Those with ambitions overseas will never gain the skills and flair that will make them employable abroad from a culture of dud films—they need the launching pad of a vibrant industry. And if Australia wants its expatriates back to reinvigorate the local scene, then the filmmaking environment here has to be such as to attract them back. Before looking ahead and speculating on future possibilities, let's briefly consider the current state of the industry.

Australia is one of the oldest filmmaking nations in the world. It was a pioneer of feature filmmaking, and has been competent at it for over 100 years.[17] Yet the defining characteristic of its history is struggle. Except for the period up to World War I, there has never been a period when Australians have not had to fight for an Australian cinema. Every achievement has been wrested from struggle against powerful exhibition and distribution giants—at one time British, and always American. Sometimes the fight has been against an indifference to our film culture on the part of both governments and the community, over long periods of time. The concerns about viability are perennial. In 1937, C.J. Dennis listed five essential requirements for a viable Australian film industry:

> (i) a regular and adequate supply of first-class stories suitable for converting into popular and therefore payable talking pictures, (ii) a fair share

of overseas business to enable the producer to recover his outlay and reap at least some profit, (iii) government assistance in some form for at least some years in the form of straight-out subsidy, if exhibition is to be confined to Australia, or a change in the law so as to provide some reciprocal arrangement with other countries, or both, (iv) sufficient capital to enable an organisation to carry on until returns come in, (v) a highly trained and efficient technical staff, sufficiently large to ensure continuous production, good business management and efficient production.[18]

Seventy years later, the fifth of these requirements has become a notable achievement. A highly trained and efficient workforce has long been realised, but there is not a critical mass sufficient to ensure continuous production. And filmmakers will recognise, with wry smiles, Dennis's modest expectation that producers might reap 'at least some profit'. Not much changes.

Despite its growth in the last 30 years, the production industry is small. Australian films are vulnerable in the face of mighty forces. This year, for instance, our lonely 15 films will stand in cinemas against 300 overseas offerings, most from the US—a barely noticeable 5% of the total number of releases. But we are not alone. All English-speaking countries struggle against the American film, because its production output is vast, and it easily able to flood the market in English-speaking countries like Australia. If only the French had kept Louisiana, and persisted with colonial expansion in the Americas, the French-language films of a Gallic Hollywood might not have overwhelmed us. Hélas for Hollywood! The US makes about 200 studio films a year, and 95% of their box office comes from domestic attendances. By contrast, local films represent 3.6% of the box office in Canada, 10% in New Zealand (boosted recently from virtually zero by the colossal success of the locally-shot *Lord of the Rings* trilogy), and 24% in Britain.[19] Australia's mere 1.6% in 2004 is woeful, but it is an historic low, and our average of around 6% in the '90s was pretty good by comparison to that of other English-speaking countries.

Nor do our films have a consistent track record of returning cost or of profitability. For instance, the FFC typically produces about half the features made in Australia. Of the 212 feature films it has produced since its establishment, nine have gone into profit, a ratio of 1:23. Mind you, Hollywood's record of success is no better than 1:10, which, although it is a kind of negative reassurance, still suggests we have plenty of room for improvement. The only long-term, consistently and highly viable part of the industry—the distribution and exhibition sector—does not, and never did, depend for its prosperity on the existence of Australian films. Not that this should be seen as a criticism; it is more in the way of a poignant comment on the structure of the industry. For filmmakers, this is not an environment conducive to making a decent living. It is a tribute to them and the industry at large that it has continued to fight for a viable industry—any industry at all—over many years, and easy to conclude that the Australian cinema is borne along by faith and oily rags.

That faith has reaped some great successes. *Crocodile*

Dundee, which took over $47 million at the box office, is the second-highest earner in Australian cinema history. It is one of only five films that have taken more than $20 million. The others are *Babe*, *Moulin Rouge*, *Crocodile Dundee 2* and *Strictly Ballroom*. Among ten films which took more than $10 million are *The Dish*, *Muriel's Wedding*, *Lantana*, *Gallipoli*, *Wog Boy* and *Shine*. Among those whose takings exceeded $5 million are *The Man Who Sued God*, *Rabbit-Proof Fence*, *Two Hands* and *Picnic at Hanging Rock*. Sixty-five films took up to $5 million including, recently, *Japanese Story*, *Strange Bedfellows*, *Getting Square* and *Somersault*.

No less impressive is the fact that Australia has built up a top-class infrastructure of studios, film services and expert personnel. The industry has been valued at $715 million, and this takes no account of the burgeoning post-production industry, which attracts more and more films here for finishing after shooting. Nick Herd has recently noted the remarkable success of Animal Logic, the Sydney-based creator of the award-winning visual effects for the *Matrix* films, 'now one of the ten leading digital-effects companies in the world'.[20] In the middle of our local crisis last year, seven foreign films were shot here, ironically, half the number of Australian films produced.[21] That Australia is attractive to overseas film interests is a welcome signal of the economic buoyancy and expertise of our world-class production infrastructure. But it also sounds a warning. If the local film falls flat on its face, all that may be left standing is a grateful foreign film industry.

Australia has a great production infrastructure, world-class expertise, a distinguished history of filmmaking, supportive governments and passionate advocates for a thriving future. What a dreadful waste it would be if such dynamic forces were to languish for want of a sound production base and good ideas. In Parts 2 and 3, some structural and conceptual changes are considered, changes which might lead to a revitalised industry.

2

Getting the structure right

The three-potato test

It is two years now since Brian Rosen was appointed chief executive officer of the Film Finance Corporation, the Australian Government's principal agency for the funding of Australian film and television production. A visionary who has been toughened by years of work as a producer in Hollywood, Rosen is thoughtful—and blunt. In as many words he has said that in the last couple of years we have made some bad films, some shallow films, that there has been a dearth of inspiring concepts, but that this must stop—now. His leadership will be about improving quality. He has no doubt that the talent is here to be fired up, and behind his words is a conviction that the industry is not in terminal decline, merely in depression. What he proposes is a revolution. Whereas in the past the FFC has acted as a bank, ensuring that the financial packages of projects have been right, Rosen is proposing—and already beginning to implement—a radical change, whereby the FFC involves itself in the quality control of those films in which it invests. In other words, the FFC will in future play an active part in creative evaluation, and monitor progress all the way from proposal to final delivery, effectively acting, not merely as bank, but also as a studio and as a distributor. There are precedents in Britain and Canada for government agencies involving themselves as thoroughly as this. Rosen's priority is to get the product right. Unless it is, there will be no financial return. And if you are able to control the product, why not take a hand in distribution and vice versa?

All this may run counter to the traditional Australian repugnance for the idea of the government agent making creative decisions. And there are always dangers in taking this path. In a deeply perceptive address to the Australian Screen Directors Association (ASDA) in 2002, Peter Sainsbury, erstwhile Head of Film Development at the AFC, appealed for a *visionary* Australian cinema—one which, he hoped, would rise above the American critic Pauline Kael's faint praise, when she likened 'watching an Australian movie to going to bed with a worthy book'.[22] Sainsbury discussed the effect of bringing film funding into what he described as the 'safe haven of the public service' after a period in the 1980s of tax rorting. He asked:

What kind of safety is this, and for whom was it

provided? Sociologists know that bureaucratic imperatives place the safety of the funding agency and the unimpeachable position of its executives before all else. So it was and is in the Australian film industry. Film financing became hostage to the three principles of bureaucracy, namely prudence, objectivity and blamelessness.

The Australia Council and its artistic constituencies are well aware of that concern, from years of skirmishes about the fairness and quality of bureaucratic decisions regarding creative life. Members of the film industry also know it well, and most would admit that in the past few people have been keen on alternative methods of peer assessment, with their attendant suspicions of conscious and unconscious bias. Yet Rosen speaks of new vision and adventurous thinking, not bureaucracy. He is nothing if not philosophical about the future. 'I'll have a fight,' he said, and has forthwith put his job on the line. If he loses, and his plans don't work, he'll walk.

Getting the product right, says Rosen, means not only ensuring that we have a product of quality, but also being clear about the budgetary market in which we are operating. We are never going to be able to compete with the US studio films and their huge $50–$100+ million dollar budgets, and it unfair and misleading to compare our situation with theirs. The more modest budgets that we are able to afford—at present we average approximately $10 million per film—mean that we do not play in the same league as the Hollywood studio industry, but in the worldwide independent-film league, a league in which budgets match our own and we can legitimately compare dramatic value for money. The much-acclaimed *Lost in Translation* was made for $6.5 million. Phillip Noyce returned from big-budget filmmaking in America in 2003 to make *Rabbit-Proof Fence* for about $9 million. Not only it has already returned its investment to the FFC, but at the time of writing is moving into profit.

Brian Rosen may have less of a fight on his hands than he imagines. For instance, Noyce is one of a number of filmmakers whose views about the size of films we should concentrate on and the quality we must strive for match Rosen's exactly. The quality of the project is the first thing to get right, he says. He was glad to get away from a system here, where the dealmaker was king and the creative worth of projects was of secondary importance:

> It was the smart operator who knew the right levers to pull, could put together the right financial deal, and who made the film, regardless of the quality of the script. Nowhere in the world could you make films that way. Someone always has to throw a dart at the wall and take responsibility for quality. You can't let market forces dictate the script.

Gillian Armstrong agrees. She remembers the 1980s and the days of the 10BA films—a tax-incentive scheme that was widely rorted—when the creative producers drifted away 'and those who could talk the talk, and walk the walk, and wear the suits, got the money'. She emphatically agrees that it is appropriate for our funding to be in the so-called Indi (i.e. Independent) range—about $2–$12 million, she thinks—and endorses the view that greater emphasis be placed on the practice of allocating limited funding to first-time filmmakers, so as to enable them to test their mettle on short, inexpensive films. Producer Lynda House points to the new AFC IndiVision Project, which she and Jocelyn Moorhouse launched for the AFC, as an inspired means of supporting low-budget features. Whereas in Hollywood it is common to pick your stars and then chase the funding, the Australian schemes of the FFC and the AFC determine budgets from the outset. 'You have three potatoes, and you have to make a meal,' she says. 'I find that an inspirational thing—and I know where I stand on the budget from the beginning.' It transforms the tyranny of the budget into a creative discipline. Producer Liz Watts of Porchlight—she made *Walking on Water*—reckons a budget allocation of around $10 million is right for the kind of films we can make best, films that place their emphasis on character development, rather than expensive special effects. Gillian Armstrong says bluntly that it is morally wrong in Australia to ask for over $20 million in funding from government film agencies, that is, from taxpayers' money. $20 million is a reasonable limit for the present size of the industry. If needed, then additional funds should be sought from private sources or from overseas. Clearly, Brian Rosen has some outspoken supporters for the changes he's proposing.

Experience and experiment

The three-tiered structure of funding films in Australia at the national level is widely regarded as world's-best practice. At the first tier, the AFC is charged with the responsibility of fostering the audiovisual production industry. It is a development agency that, through a raft of programs capped at between $20K and, until recently, about $800K, provides opportunities for newcomers and people needing experience to make small-budget films. It is also the national script-development agency. At the second tier, the FFC, responsible for funding the most expensive formats, can typically provide between $2 million and $20 million for features, though most allocations are in the order of $10 million. It would invest more if it had the resources, and finance middle-budget films. The various State film agencies and the private sector co-produce or co-invest along with the FFC. At the third tier, where budgets exceed $20 million, overseas or private-sector funding is sought to cover the balance between the FFC's upper limit and the required sum. Though no one is forced to graduate from tier to tier, the system can provide filmmakers with a staged progression over a number of years, from the first stage, at which experimental films may be made with the support of the AFC, to the lower echelons of the FFC funding—many features are made for less than $5 million—and finally up to the highest echelon where very big budgets are needed.

Experienced producers and directors working at the second tier have complained for years that inordinate funding—to which they can lay as strong a claim—has been directed towards first-feature filmmakers. Instead, they have had a desperate struggle to raise funds for their second and third projects, and at the same time maintain a professional living without long breaks between jobs. Their long layoffs are as much a brain drain as the departure of others abroad. This is especially true in the case of producers, who, as we have seen, are the high-end creative people who *do* stay in Australia, and whose expertise and experience is most sorely missed when they are absent from active production. As Lynda House ruefully observes, some top Australian producers have had to wait three years between films.

The statistics are arresting. In the last thirty years of last century, only about 10% of films were made by producers and directors with three films under their belts, and only 7% by writers of three films, whereas about 53% of producers and directors were first-timers, and nearly 66% of writers. Put another way, in the decade to 2000, 73% of producers, about 80% of directors and nearly 83% of writers made only one film, but only about 13% of producers, 7% of directors, and 3.5% of writers went on to make three or more films. It is a considerable rate of attrition.[23] And hardly surprising, perhaps, that some are asking whether funding to first-timers should be decreased and diverted to promising second-time, third-time and experienced filmmakers in order to help them further their careers. Or might this merely replenish the ranks of the expatriates and the expiring and rob the industry of fresh young aspirants?

My own view is that it should be much harder to secure funding from the FFC for a first and second feature, and I believe the Corporation will move in this direction. With the wealth of training courses available today, at secondary school and beyond, I see no reason why first-feature filmmakers should lack an understanding of visual language, the grammar of film, drama, performance or good concepts. But the last few years have demonstrated all too clearly that many do. The purpose of first features is to show promise/ brilliance with a fresh face. Two million dollars or more is a lot to outlay for first experiments or poorly-conceived projects. Nor is there any reason why we should tolerate anything less than bright, arresting first features, especially when we put so much money at Commonwealth and at State levels into tertiary training and development programs in film and broadcasting. Film is a craft of high expertise, and it is a waste of brain—and dollars—to allow aspirants through the FFC gates to take a first, or even second, step into a rigorous trade, if they are ill-prepared. Funding saved at this level could go to increase budgets for, or fund more films by, experienced teams—and so help to keep more competent filmmakers in contin-uous work.

It must be added that, contrary to all appearances, filmmaking is one of the toughest occupations in the world. It is just as well there are moment of high elation, when a film finally reaches the screen, because for many filmmakers, the three-to-five-year journey to that climactic moment has usually been arduous. In film, it is often better to arrive than to travel. So one can feel sympathy for those, especially the relative newcomers, who have had to face tough criticism in the last two years. Their commitment was never in doubt.

Meantime, at the first tier of funding, something important happened in December 2004 which might stimulate the development of better quality, more innovative first films: the AFC announced its new IndiVision program.[24] This program—in fact, it comprises five autonomous, but linked programs—is designed as an expert-supported preparation for the world of top filmmaking. Its Project lab is a professional workshop in which eight creative teams, film projects in hand, will work with leading local and overseas advisors on three areas in which weaknesses of skills and concept have been identified—script writing, performance and cinematic story-telling. There is a script-development program, a program of marketing assistance to expose filmmakers to the wider market of ideas and selling by providing travel to festivals and markets, and a program of screenings and forums showcasing outstanding low-budget films from around the world. Whatever else it achieves, this program will expose filmmakers critically to a broad range of ideas, styles and approaches to the feature film. Significantly, IndiVision will provide funds of $1 million maximum towards the making of up to three low-budget features a year, the cap of $1 million gently nudging the current $2 million lower level of FFC funding at the second tier. The introduction of all this sophisticated development, including the $1 million film fund, strengthens the argument advanced earlier, that

IndiVision might help relieve the FFC of some of the burden of its bottom-end funding, and at the same time, by monitoring the films made by the IndiVision teams for signs of promise, help to shepherd the bright ones out onto the feature platform.

Behind IndiVision lie the AFC's other continuing development projects, including programs for digital short films for newcomers, capped at $90K; a short-film program for more experienced people ($160K); short features, generally of about 15 minutes ($500K); low-budget features ($800), together with an experimental fund ($20K), and the national script development program. Reflecting on the development environment, and speaking not only of the AFC and FFC, but also of the State film agencies, Phillip Noyce believes that Australia is the best place in the world to secure script development support: 'I've had marvellous assistance from the film bodies. They have been as professional and as detailed as any studio in the world in terms of assessment quality, detail, care, promptness. It's heaven.'

I believe that there are ways in which aspects of this 'heavenly' development infrastructure can be made not only to support the Australian film industry, but also to involve expatriate filmmakers in a way that will enrich our film culture. I shall canvass this idea in Part 4.

More money, more films

The Australian film industry needs more money. Without a significant injection of private and public sector funding, it cannot continue to cultivate its own talent and attract its expatriates back home. Over the past few years private investment has all but disappeared—for want of confidence in the product and of attractive tax-based incentives. Australia's experience of tax-led investment has been heady. In the '80s, the notorious section 10BA schemes were widely rorted and fell into disrepute. Though still on the statute books, these are rarely invoked. One of Brian Rosen's avowed goals is to work with government to establish a film fund with rort-free tax incentives. Without private investment, the industry will never manage to reach up beyond the prudential limits imposed by FFC funding towards bigger budgets and more ambitious projects.

Australian film is co-dependent on government and private support. Rarely does the private or public sector alone raise the budgets for the expensive business of feature-filmmaking and, symbiotically, one acts as investment leverage for the other. Australian governments have long supported the film industry and, while the current government shows no great interest in the arts, it has nevertheless maintained a high level of appropriation for the film industry, even in its recent difficult times. The funding of IndiVision is a good example. Nevertheless, even at earlier production levels of about 20 films a year, Brian Rosen reckons it is still a cottage industry, not only because of its low output, but also because of its attendant inability to establish large viable production houses which can diversify their product to keep afloat and profitable all the time. Film critic Peter Thompson goes further. He says that at such low levels of activity we are wrong to call it 'an industry'. He refers to it, fondly and without disparagement, as a 'national film culture'. (Having defined it in this way, Thompson is angry when people decry audience support for Australian films even at the 5% attendance level of earlier years. He echoes the views of Tait Brady, one of the new assessors at the FFC: 'At this level we should be celebrating it. If 200,000 people saw *Somersault* and 500,000 people saw *Strange Bedfellows*, who's to say that's not important? In Australia, that's a good response.') However, Thompson does not support the continuation of low levels of audience response. He thinks we should increase our output to 60 films a year: 'It is destructive to set our sights as low as 20. It is not a sustainable culture at such a low temperature.' He points out that, if Hollywood's success ratio of 1:10 were to apply here, we could not expect more than 6 of the 60 films to enjoy financial success. At any rate, a high-turnover industry would also help the operation of an expatriate program.

The formula for the future is not complicated. A sustainable industry needs increased government funding, so as to coax greater private investment into a higher annual rate of production of films that will both attract and engage audiences and also return higher profits to investors.

An end to entitlement: too many filmmakers

A joke in film circles tells how St Peter welcomed Mother Teresa at the gates of heaven with the words, 'You have devoted all your life to others. Is there something now that you would like for yourself?' Mother Teresa replied that she would love to have another twenty orphanages to house her children of the streets. 'No, no,' said St Peter, 'I mean something just for yourself.' Mother Teresa paused, then said, 'Well, I've always wanted to direct.'

There are too many filmmakers in Australia. In the land of the fair go this is a tough call. Just as they have every other technology, Australians have taken up the video camera and editing packages with a passion. Everyone wants to be a filmmaker, and Australia's generous access to film-agency funding and to filmmaking courses has fuelled a sense that the industry has a place for everyone who wants one. The problem arises when would-be filmmakers overwhelm funding agencies and film schools with applications for work that is at best technically adequate, and conceptually vapid. Applicants squeeze through who shouldn't—and, little wonder, given the intense pressure.

Brian Rosen is understandably concerned: 'The sense of entitlement is crippling this industry', he says. There are so many people who have been assisted to make films, and years of greenlighting projects that were merely indifferent have created a culture of entitlement to government funds as a kind of democratic right.

The queue for funding is long. Australia has over 2000 registered companies involved in film and video production for an industry which, in good times, makes just 20 films a year. (These companies are also involved in non-feature production, of course.) In the same field, the United Kingdom, where about 80 films are made each year, has only 100 such businesses.[25] There appears to be no data available, allowing us to check the viability of these Australian companies, but it is a fair bet that many find life hard.[26] Structurally, the best way of ensuring attrition would be to implement an active policy of refusing to fund proposals of indifferent quality. It is to be hoped that this might lead, in time, to a situation in which the industry is embarrassed, not by an excess of poor proposals it *will not* fund, but by an abundance of good ones it *cannot* fund. The result should—I repeat, should—be more films of better quality made by fewer filmmakers. I shall return to the question of quality in Part 3.

A footnote on Tropfest, the world's largest, popular short-film festival, seen by about 150,000 people each year. Tropfest is a wonderfully Australian way to focus the energy of hundreds of serious and not-so-serious filmmakers, almost 800 of them this year. It is a wild gamble—last year the odds of winning the first prize were 800:1—and it is conducted with a huge sense of sport and fun. With rich prizes, and a panel of luminaries as patrons, it is beginning to attract more experienced amateurs, and even professionals. Winners have moved on to opportunities in the industry. Nevertheless, it screens the few that do have serious potential from the mass who don't, with cheerful pizazz, and deserves a place in the structural platform of the industry, with some formal monitoring and referral of promising talent.

3
Quality and diversity

Raising the bar

I t all comes down to this: quality and diversity—and the so-called 'Big E'. Quality, because no film is worth an investment cracker or an audience dollar if the product is not hot. Diversity, because audiences will not return to see the same things over and over again. The Big E stands for *Entertainment*, without which a film is nothing. Actually, I prefer *Engagement*, which implies more than entertainment or amusement for the audience, and suggests involvement and fascination, and admits films about the dark, as well as the light, side of life. The sense of entitlement held by some filmmakers has already been mentioned. Audiences, who are equal partners in the business of the cinema, have a superior entitlement—namely, to see riveting films. If film was a moral universe, then it would contain but one sin—that of being boring.

These matters will need attention in the coming

years, as they have, constantly, over the last one hundred. Perhaps, however, the downturn of the past two years will be seen as the end of a 30-year phase in the Australian feature-film industry, a period in which a world-class skills and infrastructure were established, and the Australian cinema again took a highly regarded place on the Australian and international scene. Brian Rosen certainly envisages the next few years as a second phase, in which our 'cottage industry', as he calls it, becomes a business, based on the development of intellectual property (i.e. screenplays and their realisation) of superior quality and the support of talent. Were that to be the case, why should the bar on the qualifying requirements to make a film not be set much higher than it is at present?

Insight and vision

Recent Australian films have not adequately explored the uses to which cinema's unique, rich language can be put. We are excessively reliant on narrative, and shy away from the expressive potential of metaphor and symbol and allegory. We have a cinema that tends to describe, rather than interpret. The grimness of many Australian films, especially of recent years, is not a bad thing in itself: its makers are doing what artists are supposed to do, acknowledge and explore the dark side of life as well its light. But many of these films look *at* life, rather than *into* it or *beneath its surface*. There is a reluctance to go to the hidden places, perhaps for fear of what might be discovered there. Yet film is uniquely capable of exploring the life of the mind, of visualising thought. If it is true that most Australians are less emotionally expressive in the outward sense than people of other nations, then cinema was made for us. For instance, anyone who knows the most remote regions of the outback is well aware that the loneliest places there are its vast horizons and the little chambers of the mind. Two spaces, one physical, one psychic. Cinema can explore these physical and metaphorical spaces at one and the same time. Bush people stand and gaze. Cinema loves this laconic spirit. Taking it *in*; interiority; dialogue gives way to mind-play. In no other medium can wordless experience be expressed with such power.

Some Australian filmmakers do use cinematic language beautifully. In Rolf de Heer's *Tracker*, the members of the horseback party appear as ephemeral intruders in the eternal space and time of the remote outback. He expresses timelessness in a few minutes of cinematic time, framing them as tiny creatures in wide shots for long observing takes. In the massacre scene de Heer turns time inside out. As the policeman threatens the Aboriginal people, he foregrounds the action, eerily fades the sound of the violence to the background, plays the thought track of the Tracker's recollection of the event up close and dissolves to a painting of the actual massacre—and so mixes reality, myth, present, past and future in one cinematic passage.

In his address to ASDA, Peter Sainsbury appealed for a visionary Australian cinema:

> Psychological realism, with its insistence on emotional behaviour stemming from clear causes

with logical effects and devoid of paradox, is simply inadequate to portray the chaotic, contradictory and essentially secret, even invisible machinations of desire and therefore of much human behaviour.

He asked whether what he called the 'unpretentious pragmatism' of the Australian film industry could contemplate a cinema that used the magical qualities of the medium to enlighten the political and social universe around us. Memorably, I think, he concluded that 'a film industry that does not have space, or even much respect, for the visionary will not produce internationally recognised movies of any lasting value'.

I see no reason why Australia should be incapable of producing films of richer cinematic values. But where are the filmmakers to interpret our lives in metaphor and symbol and allegory? Garry Maddox has recently observed that the Independent film movement—the middle-budget films discussed earlier—favours directors with their own way of seeing the world and with intriguing ideas.[27] The Independent Spirit Awards in the USA, which run two days before the Oscars, honour films that have 'original, provocative subject matter, uniqueness of vision and economy of means'. Those values of the Indie film are recognised worldwide. So, economically, the Australian film industry exactly fits the market model—that of the Indie film, as we have seen—which, in turn, precisely expects vision and adventure. It would be a sad irony if we finished up with the economic part of the model intact and the conceptual part in tatters.

Connecting with the life of the nation

There so many aspects of Australian life that our cinema has yet to explore. If outsiders were to judge Australia by the feature films made in the last two years, they would conclude that our society is introspective and parochial. Where are the films that look at what Paul Keating called the 'Big Picture'? 'We are a country at war,' cries Brian Rosen, 'but we have only seen one script about war.' Australia has turned the notion of refugees upside down, and made prisoners of asylum-seekers, but the FFC has received only one script on this politico-human drama. Where are the stories, serious or comedic, set against parliamentary and government life, a topic you would think was fair game among the most governed people in the world? About politics and truth? About the human dramas behind industrial relations in a time of radical change; on the monarchist/republican debate; corporate ethics; government, wood-chippers and local people on an island State; the One Nation phenomenon and a general disengagement from mainstream politics; elections; local government; the losing of the Murray; the salting of the land; and the countless other stories of the relationship between an exhausted, drought-dry land and its resilient people?

There is so much energy in Australian life, one longs to see it coursing through our films. Are we incapable of an angry cinema, an ecstatic cinema, a cinema of revelation, of political and social outrage, of the heroic and the epic? When in 2004 Louise Adler, CEO and

Publisher of Melbourne University Publishing, sought from forty leading writers responses to the military action against Saddam Hussein's regime, many refused or were reluctant to reply. I quote her at length below, because what she says of the literary world seems to match the challenges the film industry as a whole faces when it comes to the search for films of bold sweep. Having proceeded 'on the assumption that we look to writers for their responses to events of national importance because we expect them to have a view',[28] Adler was disappointed to find so few writers who were politically *engagé*:

> Stick with the local seems to be the order of the day. Avoid the Big Picture at all costs [...] Americans do the big ideas novel all the time— and they are fabulous at it [...] America allows its writers to take liberties, indeed celebrates their imaginative daring, [...] dares its writers to intellectual and creative boldness. By comparison, the Australian literary culture can appear self-referential and reluctant to take risks. [...] What is obvious is that here in Australia we cling to the ironic, the small view, to light comedy, to laconic and modest cynicism, we cling to an idea of ourselves as all rough-hewn-good-heartedness. Think of films like *The Castle,* and you will get the picture. We cling to that fantasy as tenaciously as we do to the coastline—not daring to go further into the centre.

Adler's experience, if it is also true of our cinema culture, suggests that the conceptual challenge is a big one. If the industry is to raise the value of its intellectual property, ways will have to be found to connect the Australian film to the social, cultural and political flow of the nation.

Thespian germs

Some Australian filmmakers have regarded theatre as so alien to film practice, that they have avoided it for fear of catching thespian germs. But the *principles* of the art of drama are integral to the production of narrative film. Many films have suffered from the director's lack of knowledge and experience in drama and performance. So much so that the stage and screen actor/director George Whaley has devised an Australian Film, Television & Radio School (AFTRS) directors' course called *Actorphobia: The Six-Day Cure.* Problems are compounded when directors lack understanding of dramatic structure. Audiences might not be able to give a name to the distraction they experience, but they know something's amiss when a significant character inexplicably disappears early on; or when the first fifteen minutes seem irrelevant, when the characters' relationships to one another fail to become clear; when behaviours remain implausible; when the pace and rhythm stay constant—all to no clear purpose. Aristotle's views on effective plot-structure have had wide, though by no means universal, application for a very long time: the principles of montage were understood long before Eisenstein applied them to the cinema. It is not as though guidance on these formal matters has not been readily available to contemporary young filmmakers. Film directors who associate with the theatre or who produce plays give themselves a chance to make better films, because theatre, unlike film, offers unencumbered space—and usually more time—in which to interpret dramatic intention, shape plot, develop character and hone performance. With the bar raised, there is little excuse for admitting to the professional world of narrative filmmaking anyone without dramatic knowledge or experience. There are exceptions, of course, directors with remarkable intuitive skills, who, with the right actors, create magic. But, generally, wherever performance is involved, some understanding of and sensitivity to acting and actors' ways of working are essential.

On a more practical level, theatre can be a fertile ground where filmmakers can dig out useful ideas and themes. More ideas tumble through Australian theatres in a year than can be seen on a cinema screen in a similar period. Theatregoing, especially to little, independent theatres and the fringe, can give filmmakers direct and immediate exposure to contemporary concerns, issues and lifestyles—confronting, amusing, often from unexpected spaces in Australian life. Thoughtful filmmakers not only attend the theatre, but mix with theatre people. The only germ they are likely to catch is that of a good idea.

Hard choices

There will be better Australian films when filmmakers are more knowledgeable people, who draw more for their ideas on a cultivated awareness of our literature, arts, history, social sciences, politics and all the complexities of our society. Inescapably, the quality and diversity of Australian feature films cannot be raised without requiring much, much more of applicants to film schools or those seeking film agency feature funding. Once upon a time it was enough simply to declare a passion for the cinema, and swear that filmmaking was all you ever wanted from life. But today everyone, showreels or scripts in hand, is dying to be a filmmaker. These are the ones we can eliminate first. Similarly, there is any number of well-educated and experienced people who present without a single original idea in their heads. They too can go. If you have nothing to say, don't apply. Few candidates will be left now, and schools and funding agencies may have to become accustomed to fewer people managing to jump over their newly raised bars. Rejection is painful, but just: people of indifferent talent should not be encouraged to waste precious years in, or training for, a trade at which they will probably fail. This is doubtless the direction in which Brian Rosen intends to move the FFC. AFTRS has long been toughening its criteria, and reducing its annual intake into key creative disciplines. Even so, there are still graduate films with memorable titles and forgettable content. The School is energetically addressing this problem.

What might the profile of a successful candidate for FFC funding or to AFTRS look like in future? Something like the following (and bear in mind that some Australian filmmakers lack many of these attributes and skills): a demonstrable aptitude for visual, as distinct from literary, storytelling (it is good to see AFTRS reintroducing the battery of tests for cinematic skills, similar to those used in earlier years, which successfully identified the talents of people like Gillian Armstrong, Phillip Noyce, Chris Noonan, Jocelyn Moorhouse, P.J. Hogan, and scores more); a critical interest in, and knowledge of, cinema; a lively interest and knowledge of the arts and literature, including Australian literature, and of social sciences, history, politics and the geopolitics of our region; some involvement with other performing arts, especially theatre, and a knowledge of dramatic technique and performance; imaginative, interpretive and analytical skills; life experience and a critical appreciation of it; originality, and some, but perhaps not all, of the following: vision, eccentricity, originality, obsessiveness, enthusiasm, passion, emotional resilience, leadership and humanity. And, above all—as if this weren't enough!—a point of view, something to say, something that has to be said *urgently*.

This is a formidable list of demands to make. On the other hand, what you don't ask for you'll never get. If we are going to improve the quality of the industry's intellectual property, it is not unreasonable to expect these skills to be abundantly evident in applicants for feature-film funding, and nascent in candidates for film schools.

4

An expatriate-
return program

Fresh eyes

I f the industry meets the challenges of quality and diversity discussed in Parts 2 and 3, it will re-emerge as a competitive cultural force in Australia, perhaps even in the world. When this happens, and probably not before, it could well develop an expatriate-return program which would benefit both expatriates and the home industry. It is hardly a cure for the current problems, but it would enrich a buoyant industry. Nor does it need to be tied to the Department of Foreign Affairs and Trade (DFAT), or any other department which may eventually have carriage of expatriate policies, but it would be wise for the industry to watch the course of the Senate Inquiry into Australian Expatriates, described in Part 1, and note the recommendations in its Report: there could be useful government-level support for any initiatives the industry might take itself. Similarly, the industry should look closely at the experience of the Southern Cross Group (also referred to earlier) for suggestions regarding any expatriate program plans it may itself develop. The SCG, for example, was quick to tap into expats' innate desire to keep in touch with their homeland, and, once offered, their services were taken up with extraordinary speed. At least one Australian filmmaker abroad has shared this yearning for contact with home. Phillip Noyce had not worked here for eleven years before making *Rabbit-Proof Fence*. When asked whether he had been actively looking for a screen-play that would bring him back, he replied: 'I'd been trying to find one but never with success, because I'd increasingly become unconnected with Australia. [...] You go to Hollywood and work internationally, and just the little jokes no longer make you laugh. I was alienated from my own culture.'[29] It is unthinkable that Noyce's feelings are not shared by others, who might respond readily to a formal return program. In the same vein, the industry might find it useful to monitor the SCG's recommendation to the Senate Inquiry that the Government support the establishment of a research function at an institute or university. Cooperation with such a body might add considerably to the industry's information about its diaspora.

An expatriate-return program could transform to practical purpose an ephemeral but powerful force that all our expatriates seem to share—I call it 'eucalyptus fever', an irrepressible desire to return home, not just to embrace the earth from which you were fashioned, but to create things, films, of a kind which you can make nowhere else in the world. 'Stories that run in your veins' is what Phillip Noyce called them.

There is a paradoxical attraction to offer, too, that of medium-to-small budgets. *Rabbit-Proof Fence* cost $10m, far less than the budgets of his American films, but Noyce did not see this as a disadvantage. In the US there was the never-ending struggle between the integrity of the script and the wishes of a powerful studio—all part of the game. 'I never had so much joy with all the films I've made, as I had with *Rabbit-Proof Fence*', Noyce said. 'The smaller the budget, the more it releases you to take risks. I felt free. The weight lifted off my shoulders.' These views are shared among all the expatriates with whom I have spoken over the years. So, to expatriates used to $50m+ packages, the relatively small size of the Australian budget can be presented, without apology, as an instrument of inspiration, creative freedom, exploration, and experiment, offering opportunities to explore topics and methods that may be difficult, if not impossible to tackle overseas.

The word *experiment* needs to be emphasised. Once embarked on a busy career, few filmmakers ever have the chance to experiment. It is a pity. Experiment should not only be a rite of passage for the young, but be available as an integral part of a developing career for mature filmmakers. The industry itself stands to gain from it. No step forward has ever been taken by endlessly repeating the old, and the mainstream always stands to gain from innovation. The occasional offer of experiment—to be loosely interpreted as any form of trying out, especially with ideas—in the safe haven of home might prove a strong attraction.

I suggest therefore that the FFC and the AFC together, as part of their already buoyant programs, might consider the creation of a formal, funded expatriate-return strategy in order to bring leading Australian filmmakers (and actors) home from time to time, and enable them to work, make films, experiment with both form and content, conduct workshops and teach—not only for their own benefit, but in order to channel back into the industry at home the fruits of their experience overseas. The program could make grants available for research, development and experiment at all levels, just as the existing programs do for home-based filmmakers. It goes without saying, of course, that this must not be at the expense of funds allocated to local activities. Is there any reason why returning expatriates should not engage with local filmmakers in their projects, and also make time to participate in, say, one of the continuing development activities of the AFC, and state film agencies, through attachments to expat projects, participation in workshops and hothousing—including, for example, through visiting roles in the AFC's IndiVision project? AFTRS and NIDA could be vital participants in such as scheme. Mentorship schemes, usually local, could extend to overseas, allowing expatriates not only to act as professional guides to new filmmakers in Australia, but also to those in their first year abroad, providing them a guided passage into the international sphere. A strategy of continuing contact would eventually encourage their return, too, to play the same role in developing the Australian industry as their mentors did some years before.

There are reciprocal benefits, too. Internationally, a program like this would act as an intelligence network, actively dangling *before* expatriates the bait of new writing, talent, issues, events, discoveries—whatever might resonate with their interests in Australian culture. At the same time it would respond to requests for information *from* expatriates. Through Australian diplomatic missions abroad, expatriates would be encouraged to promote the interests of Australian film and art.

These are practical benefits, but there is also a philosophical point to a proposal like this. It is to turn the notion of the homeland upside down, so that it is no longer regarded as a place of the past, to which we look back, but as a place of renewal, from which we can look forward again. When theatre director Peter Brook was asked why, several years after establishing his international theatre company in Paris, he had accepted an invitation to return to direct Shakespeare at Stratford, he replied that 'sometimes it is necessary to go back, in order to see how far you have come, and to decide how to go on'. In other words, homeland can be more than the point of departure, it can be a useful place in which to take stock, a refuelling stop on the journey, a place to enliven the spirit and recharge the batteries and do unusual or brave things.

If Australia were to follow the lead of many other countries and set up an expatriate office, such as the Australian Diaspora Council proposed by the SCG, then the film industry would stand to gain significantly from engaging with it through DFAT. This is something Government might welcome. Film and the arts have always been useful in diplomacy and trade as glamorous ambassadors. Trade follows the flag of film. Similarly, the industry can gain from the kinds of university and institute research projects conducted by Hugo, Fullilove and Flutter, and discussed earlier.

Two cautionary notes should be sounded. First, the program would have to be unbureaucratic—invisibly efficient in operation, and conspicuously easy in manner. Nothing would excite derision more among top filmmakers than the paraphernalia of applications, forms, staged processes, panels, appointments and big offices. In all likelihood it would be operated jointly by the FFC, AFC and the state film agencies. It should be run by a few wise people with wide interests and contacts. It would need to be run with the minimum of process and the maximum of contact. Secondly, it should be obligation-free, with no requirement or expectation that expatriates participate, especially to begin with. Such are the networks established by top professionals, that many will come to Australia in their own way and at their own time.

There is an overriding advantage to an expatriate-return strategy. One of the thrills of returning home after a long absence is that for a few precious months, no more, you see things with searing clarity. In their Australian films, expatriates might bring fresh eyes to show us things we can no longer see.

Conclusion: A global language

There is hope. If the film industry can rejuvenate itself to make films of high quality and great diversity at a higher level of production, then the brain drain overseas will not be seen as a threat. At the same time, that our people should look to work abroad is inevitable, something of which we can be proud, and a phenomenon which we could turn to our benefit, with savvy management of an expatriate-return program— a circular migration of talent and expertise.

To put it plainly, those who want to shoot through, will go; those who want to stay, will stay; the *only* way to keep the stayers home and entice the goers to return, is to keep stoking the furnace at home, so as to make Australia a place of vibrant originality, with better films and more production. This would transform the industry to a culturally dynamic model—one which, at the same time, provides Australians with a bold and diverse cinema created by talented filmmakers, spins some out to illustrious careers abroad, and draws them back occasionally to embrace the very qualities of the land and the industry that nurtured them to inter-national success in the first place.

The qualities that will sustain a dynamic Australian feature industry are wonderfully apparent in the lives of two filmmakers at opposite ends of the migratory cycle, local Rolf de Heer and global Phillip Noyce. De Heer went to Hollywood, but deterred by it, returned to spend his life making edgy, thoughtful, emotionally challenging films in Australia (*The Quiet Room*, *Bad Boy Bubby*, *Alexandra's Project*, *Tracker*). The financial offer he declined in America represents more money than he has ever earned from all the films he has made in the 25 years since his return. For him filmmaking is a process of immersion, in which the process— engagement with the content—is the all-important thing. 'Is the story worth telling?' he asks himself, and when it is, he describes the experience as one of joy.

Noyce spent eleven years in America, making very big-budget films. He too puts content above everything else: that—'because the story sang in his veins'—is one reason why he came back to make *Rabbit-Proof Fence* on a small budget. He too talks of the joy of making. They are separated by an ocean, and their bank balances read very differently, yet each is as content as the other in their creative lives. They epitomise the qualities in Australian filmmakers that are our marketable gold—qualities of innocent delight in the work, an absence of egotism, an unaffected enthusiasm, an uncomplicated sense of commitment, a capacity for hard work and long hours, an exhilaration with low budgets, and a greater concern with what a film has to say than with what it will earn them. Australian filmmakers also share a deep sense of humanity, and humanity speaks a global language. That's the key. At its most intensely local, an Australian film, forged in these qualities of the spirit, can unselfconsciously be a universal instrument—so much so, that watching it, people in Alice Springs or Anchorage, Baltimore or Bombay can all say, with a sigh of recognition, 'That is me. That is us. That's how it is.'

Endnotes

1 Unless otherwise indicated, film industry data and statistics are taken from the Australian Film Commission (AFC) website www.afc.gov.au The greatest number of Australian productions in the 1990s was 34, reached in 1997/98. There was a gentle decline to 2001/02, when 24 were made. In 2002/03 there were only 15, and 15 again in 2003/04.

2 These figures come from 'Igniting the Spark', a talk given by Brian Rosen in June 2004, since which time it has been estimated that by mid-2005 the percentage of box office for Australian films will have fallen further, to 1.2%.

3 'Back Home', in *The Stories of Henry Lawson*, edited by Cecil Mann (Sydney: Angus & Robertson, 1964), p. 445.

4 In Ian Britain, *Once an Australian* (Melbourne: OUP, 1997), pp. 9, 148, 149.

5 *This Dreaming Spinning Thing*, produced and directed by Storry Walton (ABC Television, 1967).

6 From the author's recollections and transcripts.

7 Among the television directors who left the ABC around 1966–68, and mainly for London were Bill Bain, Alan Burke, Dick Connolly, Ken Hannam, Tom Haydon, Tom Jeffrey, Tom Manefield, Ray Menmuir, John Power (for America), Henri Safran, David Salter,

Will Sterling, James Upshaw (eventually for Spain) and Storry Walton. Most returned.

8   At its head office, the ABC referred to Brisbane, Adelaide, Perth and Hobart by the acronym BAPH, and the states of which they were capitals as 'the Baph States'. As an adjective *Baph* suggested something wonderfully colonial and was synonymous with 'outer reaches'.

9   'Australians moving overseas', in *International Careers for Australians*, edited by Bryan Havenhand (Global Exchange, 2003). Hugo is Professor of Geography and Director of the National Key Centre for Social Applications of GIS at the University of Adelaide.

10   *Diaspora: The World-Wide Web of Australians* (Sydney: Lowy Institute for International Policy, 2004). Also available at www.lowyinstitute.org.

11   Quoted by Nick Herd, *Chasing the Runaways: Foreign film production and film studio development in Australia, 1988-2002* (Sydney: Currency House, 2004), p. 27.

12   *When are You Going to Get a Real Job? an economic study of Australian artists* by David Throsby and Devon Mills (North Sydney: Australia Council 1989) is one of a series of reports that have tracked the professional lifestyles, including incomes, of creative professionals. It represents a useful model for any future film industry data base. The Australia Council maintains detailed data on employment of artists, musicians and others in the visual and performing arts.

13   For details, see AFC website, www.afc.gov.au.

14   These figures are based on data compiled by Terence Clarke, in a NIDA working document, *A Select List of NIDA Graduates Living and/or Working Abroad* (2005).

15 Directors working overseas who are listed on the AFC's website as at April 2005 include Gillian Armstrong, Bill Bennett, Bruce Beresford, Jamie Blanks, Jane Campion, Roger Donaldson, John Duigan, Stephan Elliott, Scott Hicks, PJ Hogan, Stephen Hopkins, Mark Joffe, Gregor Jordan, Samantha Lang, Baz Luhrmann, Robert Luketic, George Miller, Jocelyn Moorhouse, Russell Mulcahy, Phillip Noyce, John Polson, Alex Proyas, Michael Rymer, Fred Schepisi, Carl Schultz, Dean Semmler, Peter Weir and Simon Wincer.

16 Estimates held by the Australian Writers Guild.

17 The world's first feature, *Soldiers of the Cross,* was produced by the Salvation Army in Melbourne in 1900, and the world's first full-length feature, *The Story of the Kelly Gang*, followed in 1906. What is arguably the world's first screenplay, *The Australian Cinematograph*, was written by Henry Lawson, possibly after seeing his first film in Sydney between 1896 and 1898, shown either by Marius Sestier, a travelling representative of the French film pioneers the Lumičre Brothers, or by Australian showmen who also operated cinematographic salons. It is written as scenes, and includes fades to black and framing descriptions. A quarter of a century before the invention of the sound film, he included an atmospheric sound track, music and a theme song. It was produced in 1971, as *Where Dead Men Lie*, from the original screenplay by Film Australia, directed by Keith Gow and produced by Gil Brealey. Between 1911 and 1913, Australia produced about one feature film a fortnight.

18 I am indebted to John Derum for drawing my attention to the Dennis reference.

19 Rosen, 'Igniting the Spark'.

20 *Chasing the Runaways*, p. 32.

21 See www.afc.gov.au Seven foreign features were shot in Australia in 2001/02 as well as in 2003/04. In each other year since 2000/01, five have been made.

22 'Visions, illusions and delusions', an address by Peter Sainsbury to the ASDA Conference, 2002

23 Figures are rounded to the nearest decimal point; see www.afc.gov.au

24 For details and updates on the IndiVision program, see www.afc.gov.au

25 Rosen, 'Igniting the Spark'.

26 It would greatly assist the understanding of the dynamics of the film industry for planning purposes, if there existed a centralised data base enabling us to track the occupational and living status of filmmakers, including their incomes, similar to that which the Australia Council has established for artists in various fields. It might usefully include details of expatriates as well. I suggest that funds be sought to add this missing link in the excellent information kept by the AFC, perhaps in collaboration with the Australian Bureau of Statistics (ABS) and any other research institutions working in the field.

27 'Small is Beautiful', *Sydney Morning Herald*, Weekend Edition, 12–13 February 2005.

28 'Open books, closed minds', *Sydney Morning Herald*, 17 December 2004. From an address to the Melbourne Writers' Festival about her experience in publishing *Authors Take Sides* (Melbourne: Melbourne University Publishing, 2004).

29 Interview with Stephen Appelbaum, see www.bbc.co.uk/films/2022/11/06/phillip_noyce_rabbit_proof_fence_interview.shtml

Readers' Forum

Deborah Klika on the mainstream and the margins

The recent papers by Julian Meyrick (*Trapped in the Past*) and Robyn Archer (*The Myth of the Mainstream*) raise some issues about the need for greater debate about how the arts are funded in Australia and our expectations of Government funding agencies.

Meyrick gives an honest and personal view of the development of theatre practice over the last thirty years. In short he claims that the cultural storm troopers of the 1970s have become the cultural gatekeepers of the noughties. It felt like Mark Davis and *Ganglands* all over again. Meyrick's analysis explains how and why the change took place and the effect on the cultural landscape. And while Meyrick may be focussed on the losses, his in particular, his paper highlights the need for a broad spectrum of artistic practice and funding that encompasses both old school processes and New Wave values. Robyn Archer's paper extends the theme; that a broad spectrum of arts practice is essential for a thriving (artistic) culture. Further, that any narrowing of that practice will ultimately produce conservative, safe, work that slowly but increasingly becomes bereft of ideas and creativity. Which brings me to this response.

Robyn Archer is right to debunk the myth of the mainstream; there should be no mainstream, but the reality is that there is only a mainstream and nothing else. We have managed to cut off (or at least under-fund) the margins, and consequently the space in between where work gets developed, supported and our identity celebrated. This space 'in between' is where many artists work, whether it be a physical or psychological or sociological space. It is where the risky, innovative and new forms of artistic practice develop and, if funded, flourish. These are the margins, where ideas bubble up from small spaces, diverse cultures, personal experiences; stories, images; performances that tell us how our society is really travelling. It is where those cultural storm troopers came from thirty years ago. Margins exist, like the mythical but real, mainstream, and each is defined by the existence of the other. It is no longer just a binary opposition of old and new; we are experiencing a shift in how art is created and experienced. A shift some describe as moving from 'models' to 'systems'; maybe from 'form' to 'process'; maybe a combination of both. Whatever the shift, it is a challenge that we all need to debate.

Which brings me to the recent Australia Council for the Arts decision to abolish the Community Cultural Development and New Media Arts Boards and fold some of the work into other Boards. In light of the broad overview and themes being articulated by Meyrick and Archer this restructure by the Council raises some questions.

The Community Cultural Development (CCD) Board and the New Media Arts Board were the two areas of Council that explored, and had connections to, those margins, those new areas of arts practice and ideas. They were the research and development arms of cultural and artistic practice. They explored processes, systems and new collaborations. The work of those Boards reflected what is increasingly becoming common artistic practice, as Archer points out—hybrid arts that cross, even refuse to be bound by, traditional boundaries. Boundaries that Archer says should be abolished. Boundaries that the Council has long recognised make it difficult for much arts practice, namely youth arts and cross-art-form work to be funded. I applaud Council in attempting to correct that difficulty with the establishment of the Inter Arts office, but would argue that such a move will not address the issue and is done at the expense of other, important, work that connects us to our culture and to the future.

The CCD field has been around for over thirty years. It is based on a philosophy and practice that reflects the deep Australian reverence for democracy, community and giving a voice to the voiceless. As a practice and philosophy it produced significant advances in artistic practice and policies such as Art and Working life, Art and Wellbeing, access and equity to the arts and support for the less-seen parts of our society. It championed and supported multicultural arts, circus performance and youth arts. It laid some fundamental philosophical frameworks for cultural development, including social capital. And while as a practice and philosophy CCD needed to be revised and re-articulated, it is a unique and distinctly Australian practice that is recognised worldwide. By abolishing the CCD Board the Council has lost an important tool that enabled it to truly shape the cultural landscape. Folding that work into other Boards has not worked previously and dilutes the focus of CCD. It is to the credit of the

CCD and New Media Arts sectors that they have managed to retain some of the programs and work in subsequent consultations.

In its defence the Council says it wants to be a strategic player in the arts, to be flexible, and to fund significant projects under the banner of Community Partnerships. Community Partnerships are an important aspect of community cultural development, often bringing large organisations and communities together. Or they can be road shows that come into town, leaving after they have done their bit. Funding them as 'lighthouse' projects means they need to be successful; to be successful they need to be risk-averse, even conservative—one of Archer's fears. But what is really surprising is where Council has now situated this work. In Marketing. The arts as commodity (and audiences as consumers). It is an easy trap believing that marketing artistic and cultural product is cultural development. It is not.

The Council has every right, in fact a duty, to revise its structure and to position itself to best serve the arts. I welcome change and applaud the Council for having the courage to try to make things better. But does this restructure reflect the cultural shift we seem to be going through? Shouldn't we be concerned that our major arts funding body has deleted the words 'new' and 'culture' from its list of Boards or divisions? What is the purpose of the restructure? To be flexible and strategic—to what end and for whom? Audiences, artists or as producers?

Of course, there is not enough money for the arts, and there is no single funding model that satisfies all parties or practices, but unless we start having debates about ideas, cultural identity, and creative practices and keep seeking the best ways that serve Australian artistic practice and the development of our culture we will end up just marketing old ideas.

Raymond Gill on myths, the mainstream and the press

Robyn Archer is such an enthusiastic advocate for the arts that one always expects a certain amount of hyperbole in her pronouncements. While her embellishments are good-naturedly accepted, if not expected, when she's spruiking an arts festival, one would expect something more researched and thought-through in an essay importantly titled *The Myth of the Mainstream: Politics and the Performing Arts in Australia Today.* Instead, she offers up a random series of thoughts and impressions, then shoehorns them into an argument about how media, government, the major arts companies and compliant audiences have allowed the 'mainstream' to swallow culture in Australia, rather like an artistic 'Blob'. Oh, why can't Australia be less like the 1950s and more like Iceland, where Archer recalls its 'phenomenal economic success [...] and that an Icelandic parent's proudest experience is seeing their offspring become a poet' (no reference given)!

While she makes some valid points about the dumbing down of culture, a lament anyone over forty living in any Western country would share, Archer overlooks some fairly obvious changes in Australia—changes she has herself brought about in her role as director of many of our arts festivals. She fails to note the proliferation of arts festivals around the country in the past twenty years, festivals that have brought work here that I would consider to be, in the main, innovative and tough. Such work has exposed audiences, critics and artists to ideas and work that they would otherwise have to travel as extensively as Archer to see. At the same time, substantial funds have been made available to festivals to commission, from local artists, new work that is precisely not the sort of 'mainstream' work we are used to seeing our state and national companies present in their annual seasons. There are now scores of artists who make work solely for festivals, not only in this country but around the world; another factor that helps bridge the gap between Australia and the rest of the world.

The success of arts festivals has contributed to what I would consider a broadening of the mainstream, as opposed to Archer's view that the arts and culture here have contracted into a bland middle ground. How else could one explain the routine acceptance by audiences and coverage by the media of areas of the arts that would once have been considered marginal?

Queer-film festivals, underground-film festivals, fringe festivals, foreign-language cinema, artist-run galleries etc. These are covered by all the broadsheet newspapers in Australia, something I believe would have been un-thinkable 15 years ago. But Archer has not even noticed that the space made available for the arts—at least in the case of the *Age*—has almost tripled over that period.

Archer has a genuine complaint when she levels criticism at some of the arts criticism published here. But, in my view, it applies to only a minority of critics, and her complaints are little different from those we hear from critics in the United States, or, to a lesser extent, the United Kingdom, where the impact of a critic is less because of their sheer number. But to compare what newspaper critics must do—communicate to the broadest audience in succinct and cogent language—to the criticism that appears in the local industry publication *RealTime*, written by and for arts practitioners, reveals how ignorant she is of the 'mainstream' media. Archer would have us believe that print arts coverage is only about arts page reviews rather than features, news stories and photographs. It might not occur to her that a page-three photograph of an artist or arts event will have far more impact on creating a culture that embraces the arts than will a thousand words of criticism.

Robyn Archer's Coda, 6 May 2005

My research into daily newspapers is extensive—pretty much every day, and sometimes, in the course of a month, in five states in Australia and three or four countries overseas. I am on planes a lot. This last month it was Tasmania, Melbourne, Adelaide and Sydney. The dominant page-three article on the arts in this period was about the Archibald Prize, a well-known and much loved portrait-painting competition. The longest piece I saw by Ray Gill—a full-page in the *Age*—was about the production/commercial aspects of *The Lion King*, which is coming to Melbourne. The most interesting were in the *Australian Financial Review*. I know exactly the demographic that a daily needs to reach, and exactly why Virginia Baxter and Keith Gallasch [of *RealTime*] made the hard personal and financial decision to create and sustain something which had the capacity to respond to art—particularly to new and adventurous art—giving it the attention that this kind of work demands.

There are many people in Australia who have stopped reading dailies because they target a potential audience for whom space, content and language are dictated by the notion of a mainstream. I believe that the very dictates Ray has outlined in his response to my essay are those corresponding to a political climate that encourages middle-of-the-road thinking and work that's on the edge and hard to deal with. I have vast experience of international festival publicists desperately trying, and frequently failing, to place stories about fantastic original local work, stories which don't stand a chance of being noticed if they are put next to a high-profile puff.

It is for exactly the same reason that many people also find the changes in the ABC disturbing. This week, having approached an ABC interview about the essay with equanimity, I was astonished to find myself in a commercial-radio-style heckle, in which I was introduced as 'grumpy' and within minutes described as 'whingeing'. Talk about being marginalised and patronised! With tiny sound bytes allowed and a nervy eye being kept on the clock, It seemed as though I was being asked why a successful entertainer— I was 'remembered' as a 'cabaret singer'—and effective artistic director whose own chutzpah could drum up audiences aplenty would find anything wrong in the world. There were moments akin to being at a drunken dinner party: 'Come on, give us an example! Where's your evidence?' A bit like Ray's demand for evidence and references.

There's evidence aplenty. Just go and talk to the legion of Australian artists who don't get offers from major arts organisations and who are scraping and working so hard to produce works of quality, that still manage to have immense appeal outside Australia. And go to Iceland and talk to people there, too—I did! You can use the internet to research their economy.

I titled my essay *The Myth of the Mainstream*. The important-sounding subtitle: 'politics and the performing arts in Australia today' was added by the editor, and too late for me to argue about the dangers of seeming self-importance. And I would be inclined to take to heart accusations of being grumpy, ignorant, a whinger and poor researcher, were it not for the large gatherings I recently addressed in London, Hobart, Sydney and Melbourne, where the very kinds of things I said in the essay, and expressed in exactly the same tone, were greeted with prolonged applause and rewarded with further invitations.

Contributors

Deborah Klika

Deborah Klika trained at the ABC and has worked in film, television and video production. She was a member of the Australia Council for the Arts 1997–2002, serving as Chair of the Community Cultural Development Board, Multicultural Arts Committee, and Youth Arts Panel. She is currently doing postgraduate research in Australian TV comedy.

Raymond Gill

Ray Gill is arts editor of the *Age* newspaper, Melbourne.

Robyn Archer

Robyn Archer's Platform Paper, *The Myth of the Mainstream: Politics and the Performing Arts in Australia Today*, was published in April.

Subscribe to **Platform Papers**

Individual recommended retail price: $12.95

Have the papers delivered quarterly to your door:
4 ISSUES FOR $48.00 INCLUDING POSTAGE WITHIN AUSTRALIA

To Currency House Inc.
Please start this subscription from this issue/the next issue.

Name_____

Address_____

_____

State _____ Postcode _____

Email _____

Telephone _____

Please make cheques payable to Currency House Inc.

Or charge: ___ Mastercard ___ Bankcard ___ Visa

Card no. ___ ___ ___ ___   ___ ___ ___ ___

___ ___ ___ ___   ___ ___ ___ ___   Expiry date _____

Signature _____

CURRENCY HOUSE

Fax this form to: Currency House Inc. at 02 9319 3649

Or post to: PO Box 2270, Strawberry Hills NSW 2012 Australia